World's Greatest Sports Stars The World's Greatest Sports Stars
World's Greatest Sports Stars The World's Greatest Sports Stars
World's Greatest Sports Stars The World's Greatest Sports Stars

Sports Illustrated KIDS

S0-BDO-398

The World's Greatest
Football Players

by Matt Doeden

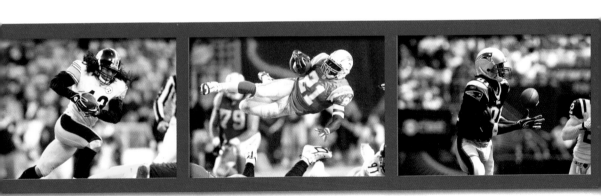

CAPSTONE PRESS
a capstone imprint

Sports Illustrated KIDS The World's Greatest Sports Stars is published by Capstone Press,
151 Good Counsel Drive, P.O. Box 669, Mankato, Minnesota 56002.
www.capstonepub.com

Books published by Capstone Press are manufactured with paper
containing at least 10 percent post-consumer waste.

Library of Congress Cataloging-in-Publication Data
Doeden, Matt.
    The world's greatest football players / by Matt Doeden.
    p. cm. — (Sports Illustrated Kids)
    Includes bibliographical references and index.
    Summary: "Describes the achievements and career statistics of football's
greatest stars" — Provided by publisher.
    ISBN 978-1-4296-3924-8 (library binding)
    ISBN 978-1-4296-4871-4 (paperback)
    1. Football players — Biography — Juvenile literature. 2. Football players.
I. Title. II. Series.
GV939.D64A3 2010
796.332092'2 — dc22
[B]   2009028536

Editorial Credits

Aaron Sautter, editor; Tracy Davies, designer; Eric Gohl, media researcher;
    Laura Manthe, production specialist

Photo Credits

Shutterstock/Ksash, backgrounds
Sports Illustrated/Al Tielemans, 26; Bill Frakes, 15; Bob Rosato, 4–5 (background),
    30–31 (background); Damian Strohmeyer, 1 (right), 5 (left, right), 11, 16, 20;
    David E. Klutho, cover; John Biever, 1 (left), 19, 22; John W. McDonough,
    4 (left, right), 12, 25; Peter Read Miller, 8; Robert Beck, 1 (center), 7;
    Simon Bruty, 29

Statistics in this book are current through the 2008 NFL season.

Printed in the United States of America in Stevens Point, Wisconsin.
062011   006228WZVMI

Table of Contents

Go Deep!

Whoosh! Tom Brady chucks a deep bomb down the field. Smack! DeMarcus Ware slams into a quarterback for a sack. Each week, excited football fans pack stadiums to watch high-flying offenses and smashmouth defenses. The National Football League's (NFL's) greatest players don't disappoint. Fans are thrilled when their favorite players hit the gridiron.

great **catches**   blinding **speed**

pinpoint **passes**

crushing **tackles**

Regular Season Rushing Stats

Year	Team	Games	Rushes	Yards	Avg.	TD
2001	SDG	16	339	1,236	3.6	10
2002	SDG	16	372	1,683	4.5	14
2003	SDG	16	313	1,645	5.3	13
2004	SDG	15	339	1,335	3.9	17
2005	SDG	16	339	1,462	4.3	18
2006	SDG	16	348	1,815	5.2	28
2007	SDG	16	315	1,474	4.7	15
2008	SDG	16	292	1,110	3.8	11
CAREER		**127**	**2,657**	**11,760**	**4.4**	**126**

(Avg. = average yards per run; TD = rushing touchdowns)

achievements

Pro Bowl selection: 2002, 2004, 2005,
    2006, 2007
NFL MVP: 2006
NFL record for combined rushing and
    receiving touchdowns (31): 2006
NFL rushing leader: 2006, 2007
Has thrown seven touchdown passes in
    his career

fact

Tomlinson's 100th career touchdown came in his 89th game. He reached that mark faster than any player in NFL history.

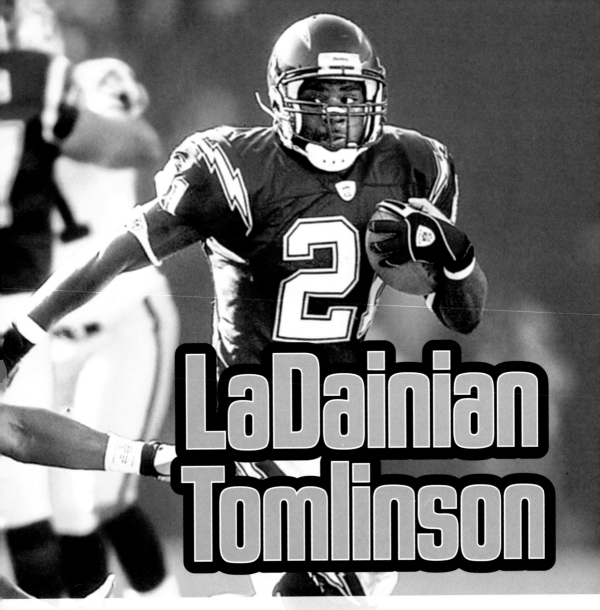

LaDainian Tomlinson

LaDainian Tomlinson is a true double threat. He's a quick and powerful runner for the San Diego Chargers. His strong, soft hands also make him a great receiver. Tomlinson has blazed through the NFL since his rookie year in 2001. Tomlinson's best season was in 2006. He rushed for 1,815 yards and scored a record 31 total touchdowns. He was named the NFL's Most Valuable Player (MVP) that year.

Dwight Freeney

When Dwight Freeney makes a spin move, the quarterback is in trouble. Freeney's speed-rushing style creates chaos at the **line of scrimmage**. As a rookie in 2002, he burst into the NFL with 13 **sacks**. He has been hammering quarterbacks ever since. Freeney helped the Indianapolis Colts win the Super Bowl in 2007.

Regular Season Defensive Stats

Year	Team	Games	Tackles	Sacks	FF	FR	TD
2002	IND	16	41	13.0	9	1	0
2003	IND	15	31	11.0	4	2	1
2004	IND	16	34	16.0	4	0	0
2005	IND	16	34	11.0	6	0	0
2006	IND	16	26	5.5	4	0	0
2007	IND	9	18	3.5	4	0	0
2008	IND	15	24	10.5	4	0	0
CAREER		103	208	70.5	35	3	1

(FF = forced fumbles; FR = fumble recoveries; TD = defensive touchdowns)

achievements

Pro Bowl selection: 2003, 2004, 2005, 2008
First-Team All-Pro selection: 2004, 2005
Super Bowl champion: 2007
NFL sack leader (16), 2004
All-time Indianapolis Colts sack leader

line of scrimmage: the line where the football is placed at the start of each play

sack: a tackle of the quarterback behind the line of scrimmage

fact In high school, Freeney was an all-around great athlete. He earned letters in football, baseball, basketball, and soccer.

Name: Thomas Edward Brady Jr.
Born: August 3, 1977, in San Mateo, California
College: University of Michigan
Height: 6 feet, 4 inches
Weight: 225 pounds
Position: Quarterback

Regular Season Passing Stats

Year	Team	Games	Att.	Comp.	Yards	TD	Int.
2000	NE	1	3	1	6	0	0
2001	NE	15	413	264	2,843	18	12
2002	NE	16	601	373	3,764	28	14
2003	NE	16	527	317	3,620	23	12
2004	NE	16	474	288	3,692	28	14
2005	NE	16	530	334	4,110	26	14
2006	NE	16	516	319	3,529	24	12
2007	NE	16	578	398	4,806	50	8
2008	NE	1	11	7	76	0	0
CAREER		113	3,653	2,301	26,446	197	86

(Att. = passing attempts; Comp. = completions;
TD = touchdown passes; Int. = interceptions)

achievements

Pro Bowl selection: 2001, 2004, 2005, 2007
NFL Most Valuable Player: 2007
Super Bowl champion: 2001, 2003, 2004
Super Bowl MVP: 2001, 2003
NFL record 50 touchdown passes in 2007

fact

In 2008, Brady hurt his knee in the first game of the season. He needed surgery and missed the rest of the year.

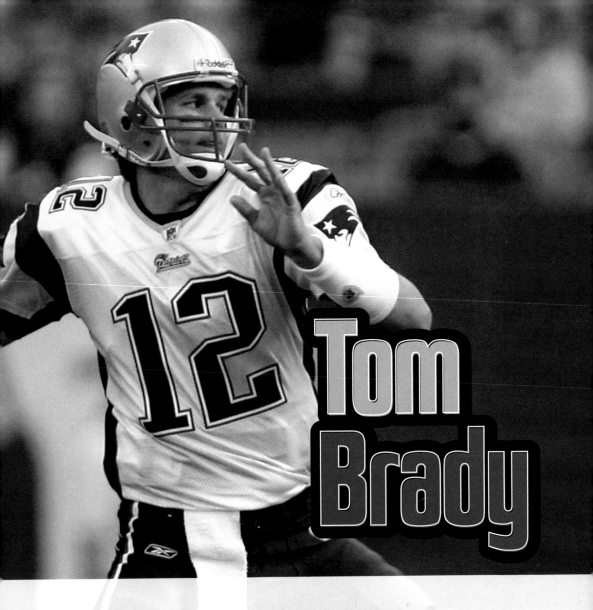

Tom Brady

Tom Brady always knows how to pick apart a defense. He can find holes in the line or hit his receivers deep. Brady barely played in his first season. But he burst onto the NFL scene in 2001. He led the New England Patriots to the Super Bowl championship. It was just the first of three Super Bowl titles. In 2007, Brady tossed an amazing record 50 touchdown passes!

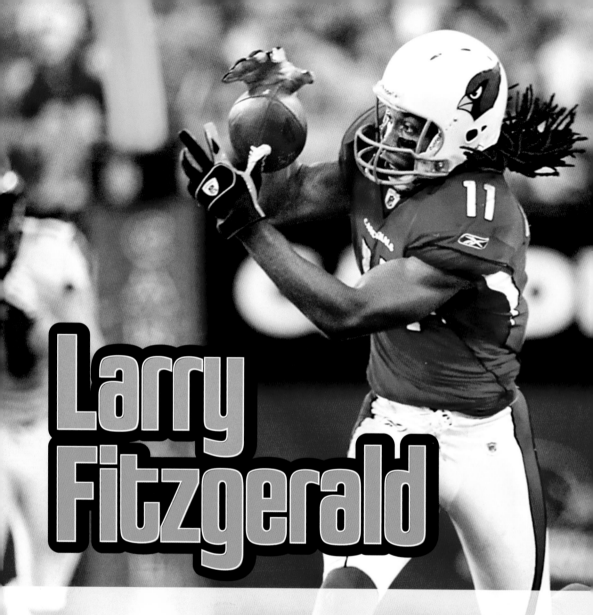

Larry Fitzgerald

Larry Fitzgerald can catch almost any pass. He is big and strong, and has great hands. He can jump higher than most defenders. In 2005, Fitzgerald led the league with 103 **receptions**. Fitzgerald was on fire in 2008. He grabbed a record seven touchdown catches in the playoffs. His steady hands led the Arizona Cardinals to the Super Bowl that year.

personal information

Name: Larry Darnell Fitzgerald Jr.
Born: August 31, 1983, in Minneapolis, Minnesota
College: University of Pittsburgh
Height: 6 feet, 3 inches
Weight: 217 pounds
Position: Wide Receiver

Regular Season Receiving Stats

Year	Team	Games	Catches	Yards	Avg.	TD
2004	ARI	16	58	780	13.4	8
2005	ARI	16	103	1,409	13.7	10
2006	ARI	13	69	946	13.7	6
2007	ARI	15	100	1,409	14.1	10
2008	ARI	16	96	1,431	14.9	12
CAREER		76	426	5,975	14.0	46

(Avg. = average yards per catch; TD = receiving touchdowns)

achievements

Pro Bowl selection: 2005, 2007, 2008
First-Team All-Pro selection: 2008
Led NFL in catches (103) in 2005
Tied for NFL lead in touchdown catches
      (12) in 2008
Won college football's Biletnikoff Award in
      2003 as the nation's best wide receiver
Set NFL records for catches (30), yards (546),
      and touchdown catches (7) in a single
      postseason in 2009

reception: a catch
of a forward pass

fact | As a teenager, Fitzgerald worked as a ball boy
for the Minnesota Vikings.

Regular Season Passing Stats

Year	Team	Games	Att.	Comp.	Yards	TD	Int.
2001	SDG	1	27	15	221	1	0
2002	SDG	16	526	320	3,284	17	16
2003	SDG	11	356	205	2,108	11	15
2004	SDG	15	400	262	3,159	27	7
2005	SDG	16	500	323	3,576	24	15
2006	NOR	16	554	356	4,418	26	11
2007	NOR	16	652	440	4,423	28	18
2008	NOR	16	635	413	5,069	34	17
CAREER		107	3,650	2,334	26,258	168	99

(Att. = passing attempts; Comp. = completions;
TD = passing touchdowns; Int. = interceptions)

achievements

Pro Bowl Selection: 2004, 2006, 2008
Comeback Player of the Year: 2004
Offensive Player of the Year: 2008
Led NFL in passing yards: 2006, 2008
Big Ten Conference MVP: 2000

fact

In 2008, Brees passed for 300 or more yards in 10 games. He was only the second quarterback in NFL history to hit that mark.

Drew Brees

Defenses often struggle to stop Drew Brees. The New Orleans Saints quarterback has a cannon for an arm. He's strong, accurate, and one of the best passers in the game. In 2008, Brees passed for 5,069 yards. It was the second highest total in NFL history. He barely missed Dan Marino's record of 5,084 yards.

James Harrison

James Harrison had to earn his playing time. He wasn't even drafted out of college. But the Pittsburgh Steelers' linebacker really shines in big games. In the 2009 Super Bowl, he **intercepted** a pass at the goal line. He ran it back 100 yards for the longest touchdown in Super Bowl history. Harrison was named the NFL's Defensive Player of the Year in 2008.

Name: James Harrison Jr.
Born: May 4, 1978, in Akron, Ohio
College: Kent State University
Height: 6 feet
Weight: 242 pounds
Position: Linebacker

Regular Season Defensive Stats

Year	Team	Games	Tackles	Sacks	Int.	FF	TD
2002	PIT	1	0	0.0	0	0	0
2004	PIT	16	36	1.0	0	0	1
2005	PIT	16	36	3.0	1	0	0
2006	PIT	11	14	0.0	0	0	0
2007	PIT	16	76	8.5	1	7	0
2008	PIT	15	67	16.0	1	7	0
CAREER		75	229	28.5	3	14	1

(Int. = interceptions; FF = forced fumbles;
TD = defensive touchdowns)

achievements

Pro Bowl selection: 2007, 2008
NFL Defensive Player of the Year: 2008
First-team All-Pro: 2008
Super Bowl champion: 2006, 2009
Holds Super Bowl record for longest play with a
    100-yard touchdown

intercept: to catch a pass made by the opposing quarterback

fact
Harrison played mostly on special teams early in his career. He didn't become a full-time starter until 2007.

Regular Season Passing Stats

Year	Team	Games	Att.	Comp.	Yards	TD	Int.
1998	IND	16	575	326	3,739	26	28
1999	IND	16	533	331	4,135	26	15
2000	IND	16	571	357	4,413	33	15
2001	IND	16	547	343	4,131	26	23
2002	IND	16	591	392	4,200	27	19
2003	IND	16	566	379	4,267	29	10
2004	IND	16	497	336	4,557	49	10
2005	IND	16	453	305	3,747	28	10
2006	IND	16	557	362	4,397	31	9
2007	IND	16	515	337	4,040	31	14
2008	IND	16	555	371	4,002	27	12
CAREER		**176**	**5,960**	**3,839**	**45,628**	**333**	**165**

(Att. = passing attempts; Comp. = completions;
TD = passing touchdowns; Int. = interceptions)

achievements

Pro Bowl selection: 1999, 2000, 2002,
    2003, 2004, 2005, 2006, 2007, 2008
Pro Bowl MVP: 2005
NFL MVP: 2003, 2004, 2008
Super Bowl MVP: 2007
Indianapolis Colts all-time leader in
    passing yards and passing touchdowns

fact | Peyton's brother, Eli, plays quarterback for the New York Giants. Eli led the Giants to a Super Bowl win in 2008.

Peyton Manning

When Peyton Manning drops back to pass, defenses are in trouble. Manning has a strong arm and a great feel for the game. He can find open receivers anywhere on the field. Manning was the top pick of the 1998 NFL Draft. Since then, he's been the league's MVP three times. In 2004, Manning threw a record 49 touchdown passes. In 2007, he led the Indianapolis Colts to the Super Bowl championship.

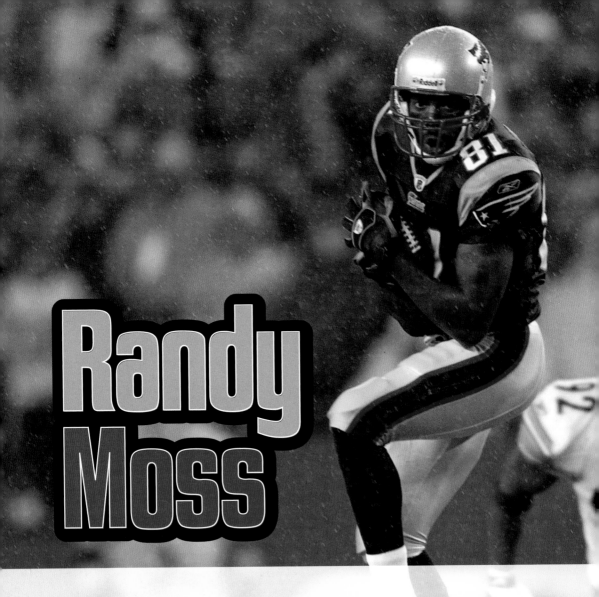

Randy Moss

Few receivers can match Randy Moss' speed, leaping ability, and steady hands. Moss lit up the NFL in 1998. He set a rookie record with 17 touchdown catches for the Minnesota Vikings. Moss has kept defenses on their toes ever since. In 2007, he set an amazing NFL record with 23 touchdown catches in a season. He helped lead the New England Patriots to an undefeated regular season.

Name: Randall Gene Moss
Born: February 13, 1977, in Rand, West Virginia
College: Marshall University
Height: 6 feet, 4 inches
Weight: 210 pounds
Position: Wide Receiver

Regular Season Receiving Stats

Year	Team	Games	Catches	Yards	Avg.	TD
1998	MIN	16	69	1,313	19.0	17
1999	MIN	16	80	1,413	17.7	11
2000	MIN	16	77	1,437	18.7	15
2001	MIN	16	82	1,233	15.0	10
2002	MIN	16	106	1,347	12.7	7
2003	MIN	16	111	1,632	14.7	17
2004	MIN	13	49	767	15.7	13
2005	OAK	16	60	1,005	16.8	8
2006	OAK	13	42	553	13.2	3
2007	NE	16	98	1,493	15.2	23
2008	NE	16	69	1,008	14.6	11
CAREER		170	843	13,201	15.7	135

(Avg. = average yards per catch; TD = receiving touchdowns)

achievements

Pro Bowl selection: 1998, 1999, 2000,
    2002, 2003, 2007
NFL Offensive Rookie of the Year: 1998
NFL rookie record 17 receiving touchdowns
    in 1998
NFL record 23 receiving touchdowns in 2007
Pro Bowl record 212 receiving yards in 1999

fact

Moss has thrown eight passes in his NFL career. He completed four of them. Two of them went for touchdowns.

DeMarcus Ware

Many quarterbacks fear DeMarcus Ware. Since entering the NFL in 2005, the Dallas Cowboys linebacker has been a sack machine. His sack total has increased every season. In 2008, he buried the quarterback a jaw-dropping 20 times! Ware is also an expert at jarring the ball loose. Opposing quarterbacks often **fumble** the ball when he slams them to the ground.

Regular Season Defensive Stats

Year	Team	Games	Tackles	Sacks	Int.	FF	TD
2005	DAL	16	47	8.0	0	3	0
2006	DAL	16	59	11.5	1	5	2
2007	DAL	16	60	14.0	0	4	0
2008	DAL	16	69	20.0	0	6	0
CAREER		64	235	53.5	1	18	2

(Int. = interceptions; FF = forced fumbles;
TD = defensive touchdowns)

achievements

Pro Bowl selection: 2006, 2007, 2008
First-Team All-Pro selection: 2007, 2008
NFL sack leader (20.0) in 2008
Butkus Award winner as NFL's best
linebacker: 2008
Sun Belt Conference Defensive Player
of the Year: 2004

fumble: when a player drops the ball while trying to move it forward on the field

fact

In 2008, Ware tied an NFL record by getting at least one sack for 10 straight games.

personal information

Name: Adrian Lewis Peterson
Born: March 21, 1985, in Palestine, Texas
College: University of Oklahoma
Height: 6 feet, 1 inch
Weight: 217 pounds
Position: Running Back

Regular Season Rushing Stats

Year	Team	Games	Rushes	Yards	Avg.	TD
2007	MIN	14	238	1,341	5.6	12
2008	MIN	16	363	1,760	4.8	10
CAREER		**30**	**601**	**3,101**	**5.2**	**22**

(Avg. = average yards per run; TD = rushing touchdowns)

achievements

Pro Bowl selection: 2007, 2008
Pro Bowl MVP: 2007
Offensive Rookie of the Year: 2007
NFL record 296 rushing yards in a game:
    November 4, 2007, vs. San Diego Chargers
Best Breakthrough Athlete ESPY award: 2008

fact Peterson's nickname is A.D., which stands for "All Day."

Adrian Peterson

The Minnesota Vikings' Adrian Peterson is a threat to score any time he touches the ball. His speed, power, and vision are unmatched. Peterson took the NFL by storm as a rookie in 2007. In just his eighth game, Peterson set the single game rushing record with 296 yards! Peterson had an even better season in 2008. He led the NFL in rushing with 1,760 yards.

Troy Polamalu

It's hard to miss Troy Polamalu on the football field. Opposing teams are always watching for his famous long, curly hair. Polamalu's speed and strength make him one of the best defenders in the game. The Pittsburgh Steelers safety is great at containing the passing game. He's even better at **blitzing** the quarterback. Polamalu is a two-time Super Bowl champ and a five-time Pro Bowler.

Regular Season Defensive Stats

Year	Team	Games	Tackles	Sacks	Int.	TD
2003	PIT	16	30	2.0	0	0
2004	PIT	16	67	1.0	5	1
2005	PIT	16	73	3.0	2	1
2006	PIT	13	58	1.0	3	0
2007	PIT	11	45	0.0	0	0
2008	PIT	16	54	0.0	7	0
CAREER		88	327	7.0	17	2

(Int. = Interceptions; TD = Defensive touchdowns)

achievements

Pro Bowl selection: 2004, 2005, 2006,
    2007, 2008
Super Bowl champion: 2006, 2009
NFL record three sacks in one game by a
    safety: 2005
University of Southern California team MVP
    in 2001
College All-American first team in 2001

blitz: when a defender who usually does not rush the quarterback does so

fact

Polamalu's uncle Kennedy Pola coaches running backs for the Jacksonville Jaguars.

Name: Edward Earl Reed
Born: September 11, 1978, in St. Rose, Louisiana
College: University of Miami
Height: 5 feet, 11 inches
Weight: 200 pounds
Position: Safety

Regular Season Defensive Stats

Year	Team	Games	Tackles	Sacks	Int.	TD
2002	BAL	16	71	1.0	5	1
2003	BAL	16	59	1.0	7	3
2004	BAL	16	62	2.0	9	2
2005	BAL	10	33	0.0	1	0
2006	BAL	16	51	0.0	5	1
2007	BAL	16	29	0.0	7	1
2008	BAL	16	34	1.0	9	3
CAREER		106	339	5.0	43	11

(Int. = interceptions; TD = defensive touchdowns)

achievements

Pro Bowl selection: 2003, 2004, 2006,
    2007, 2008
Defensive Player of the Year: 2004
NFL leader in interceptions: 2004 (9)
    and 2008 (9)
Baltimore Ravens' all-time leader in
    interceptions (43)
Unanimous 2008 All-Pro (the only unanimous
    selection in the NFL)

fact

In 2004, Reed set a record by scoring a
106-yard touchdown after an interception.
In 2008, he broke his own record by
scoring from 108 yards away!

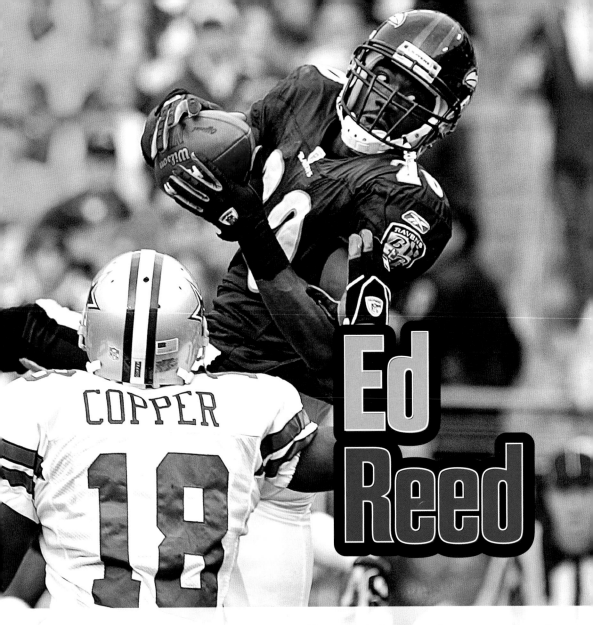

Ed Reed

Ed Reed is always trying to get his hands on the football. The Baltimore Ravens safety loves causing chaos on the field. Reed has scored many touchdowns on defense and special teams. He's scored on interceptions, fumbles, blocked punts, and punt returns. Reed's skills have made him one of the NFL's all-time great defenders.

Glossary

blitz (BLITS) — a play in which a defender who does not normally rush the quarterback does so

draft (DRAFT) — the process of choosing a person to join a sports organization or team

fumble (FUHM-buhl) — when a player drops the ball while trying to advance it forward on the field

gridiron (GRID-eye-urn) — a football field

intercept (in-tur-SEPT) — to catch a pass made by the opposing quarterback

line of scrimmage (LINE UHV SKRIM-ij) — an imaginary line upon which the football is placed at the beginning of each play

reception (ri-SEP-shuhn) — when a player catches a forward pass

rookie (RUK-ee) — a first-year player

sack (SAK) — when a defensive player tackles the opposing quarterback behind the line of scrimmage

undefeated (un-dee-FEE-tuhd) — when a team or player wins every game in a season

Read More

Buckman, Virginia. *Football Stars*. Sports Stars. New York: Children's Press, 2007.

Doeden, Matt. *The Best of Pro Football*. Best of Pro Sports. Mankato, Minn.: Capstone Press, 2010.

Dougherty, Terri. *The Greatest Football Records*. Sports Records. Mankato, Minn.: Capstone Press, 2009.

Smithwick, John. *Meet Peyton Manning: Football's Top Quarterback*. All-Star Players. New York: PowerKids Press, 2007.

Internet Sites

FactHound offers a safe, fun way to find Internet sites related to this book. All of the sites on FactHound have been researched by our staff.

Here's all you do:

Visit *www.facthound.com*

FactHound will fetch the best sites for you!

Index